MEASURE IT!

Measuring Volume

By T. H. Baer

Gareth Stevens
PUBLISHING

Please visit our website, www.garethstevens.com. For a free color catalog of all our high-quality books, call toll free 1-800-542-2595 or fax 1-877-542-2596.

Library of Congress Cataloging-in-Publication Data

Baer, T. H., author.
 Measuring volume / T. H. Baer.
    pages cm. — (Measure it!)
ISBN 978-1-4824-3872-7 (pbk.)
ISBN 978-1-4824-3873-4 (6 pack)
ISBN 978-1-4824-3874-1 (library binding)
1. Volume (Cubic content)—Measurement—Juvenile literature. 2. Measurement—Juvenile literature. I. Title. II. Series: Measure it! (Gareth Stevens Publishing)
 QC104.B34 2016
 516.1—dc23

                                  2015031500

Published in 2016 by
Gareth Stevens Publishing
111 East 14th Street, Suite 349
New York, NY 10003

Designer: Laura Bowen
Editor: Ryan Nagelhout

Photo credits: Cover, pp. 1, 7 (bottom) Kidstock/Blend Images/Getty Images; pp. 2-24 (background texture) style_TTT/Shutterstock.com; p. 5 Stephen Swain Photography/ The Image Bank/Getty Images; p. 7 (bread) Binh Thanh Bui/Shutterstock.com; p. 7 (quarters) Abel Tumik/Shutterstock.com; p. 9 Steve Wisbauer/Photolibrary/ Getty Images; p. 11 (gallon) J. Gatherum/Shutterstock.com; p. 11 (quart) Dejan Stanisavljevic/Shutterstock.com; p. 13 (juice) Vlue/Shutterstock.com; p. 13 (teaspoon) Lonely Walker/Shutterstock.com; p. 15 Stewart Sutton/Stone/Getty Images; pp. 17, 19 (beakers) PRILL/Shutterstock.com; p. 19 (rock) Grimgram/Shutterstock.com; p. 21 Monkey Business Images/Shutterstock.com.

Printed in the United States of America

CPSIA compliance information: Batch #CW16GS: For further information contact Gareth Stevens, New York, New York at 1-800-542-2595.

Contents

Finding the Space 4

The Units. 6

Buying Volume 10

Measuring Metric. 12

Odd Objects. 14

Other Units. 20

Glossary. 22

For More Information. 23

Index. 24

Boldface words appear in the glossary.

Finding the Space

Volume is the amount of space an object takes up. All objects have volume. You can measure volume in many different ways. Measuring volume can often be hard if an object has a weird shape.

The Units

Volume can be measured using many different **units**. In the United States, the most common measurement of volume is the fluid ounce (fl oz). You may know the ounce as a unit used to measure the weight of solids, but the fluid ounce is used to measure liquid volume.

1 ounce (weight) =

a slice of bread   or   5 quarters

1 fluid ounce (volume) =

a small cup
of medicine

7

Other measurements of volume include teaspoons (tsp) and tablespoons (tbsp). They can be **converted** to other units. One fluid ounce is equal to 2 tablespoons. A fluid ounce is also equal to 6 teaspoons. A cup (c) is 8 fluid ounces, while 2 cups are a pint (pt).

1 fl oz	=	2 tablespoons or 6 teaspoons

1 cup	=	8 fl oz or 16 tablespoons

1 cup

1 tablespoon

1 teaspoon

9

Buying Volume

Many things at the store are sold using volume measurements. Milk is sold in quarts (qt) or gallons (gal). A quart of milk is 2 pints or 4 cups. A gallon of milk is 4 quarts. This is equal to 8 pints or 16 cups.

1 gallon = 4 quarts

quart

=

gallon

Measuring Metric

In other countries, metric measurements are used for volume. A milliliter (ml) measures liquid on a very small **scale**. It's equal to about 20 drops of water. One teaspoon is equal to about 5 milliliters of liquid. A liter (L) is made of 1,000 milliliters!

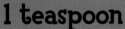
1 teaspoon

1 liter of juice

conversions

US measurements		metric measurements
1 teaspoon	=	about 5 ml
1 fluid ounce	=	about 30 ml
1 cup	=	about 237 ml

Odd Objects

A **graduated cylinder** measures liquid volume. Marks on the side of a graduated cylinder measure the amount of liquid inside. You can use a graduated cylinder to find the volume of solid objects, too.

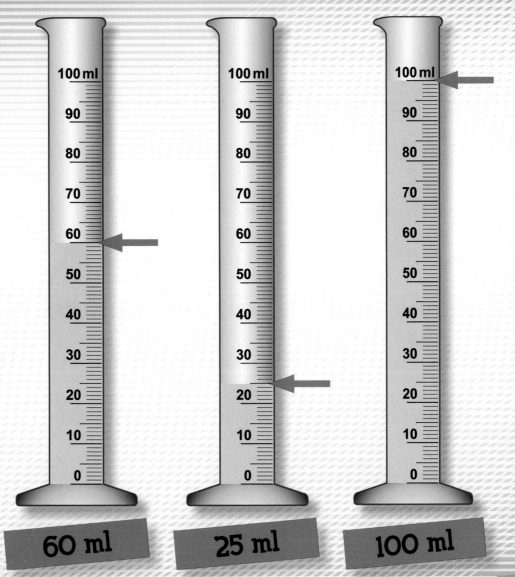

60 ml

25 ml

100 ml

Fill a graduated cylinder partly with water. Place a solid object in the water. The difference between the measurement shown after the object is in the cylinder and the measurement shown before is the volume of the object.

Let's measure the volume of this rock. The graduated cylinder has 10 milliliters of water in it. After the rock is put into the cylinder, the cylinder measures 20 milliliters. If you subtract the amount of water you first measured, you know the rock has a volume of 10 milliliters!

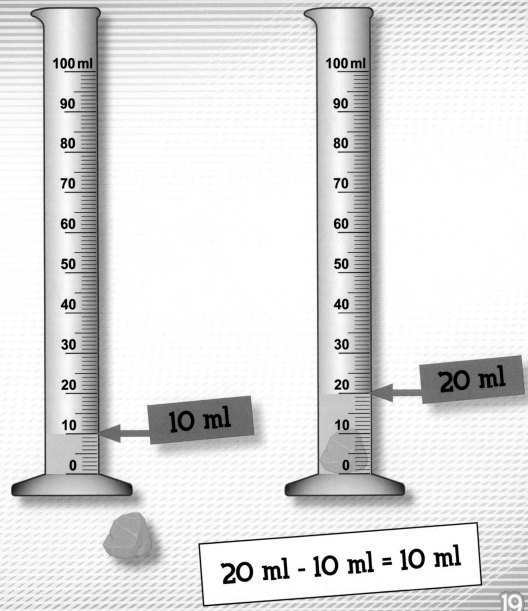

100 ml

90

80

70

60

50

40

30

20

10

0

10 ml

100 ml

90

80

70

60

50

40

30

20

10

0

20 ml

20 ml - 10 ml = 10 ml

19

Other Units

Lots of different units can be used to measure volume. The next time you're at the grocery store, see how many things you can find that are measured in volume!

Glossary

convert: to change from one unit to another

graduated cylinder: a tall, narrow holder that has measurements marked on it and is used to measure liquid volume

scale: size in relation to another thing

unit: a uniform amount used for measuring

For More Information

Books

Gardner, Robert. *How Big Is Big? Science Projects with Volume*. Berkeley Heights, NJ: Enslow Elementary, 2015.

Heos, Bridget. *What Are Measurements?* New York, NY: Britannica Educational Publishing, 2015.

Reinke, Beth Bence. *Measuring Volume*. Ann Arbor, MI: Cherry Lake Publishing, 2014.

Websites

Exploring Measurement—Volume
science-notebook.com/measure02-vol.html
Learn more about the units we use to measure volume.

Kids Math: Finding the Volume of a Cube or Box
ducksters.com/kidsmath/finding_the_volume_of_a_cube_or_box.php
Find out how to measure the volume of a cube or box with this site.

Measuring Volume Using a Graduated Cylinder
wisc-online.com/learn/natural-science/chemistry/gch302/measuring-volume-using-a-graduated-cylinder
Learn how to use a graduated cylinder to measure volume here.

Index

cup 8, 10

fluid ounce 6, 8

gallons 10

graduated cylinder
      14, 16, 18

liter 12

metric measurements
      12

milliliter 12, 18

pint 8, 10

quarts 10

tablespoons 8

teaspoons 8, 12

units 6, 8, 20